Dedication

Special thanks to Beth Hauser and Krista Downing who
labored over this text.

Eternal thanks to Jesus Christ, my Savior, who looked out
into eternity, He saw where we were all headed and chose
to go to the cross. Why? Because He could not bear the
thought of spending eternity without us.

Navigating Life Series

Psalm 23 – Fall 2010

THIS SERIES
Will do you no good unless you read it.

THIS SERIES
Will do you limited good if you only read it.

THIS SERIES
Could do you great good if you participated fully in the
small group experience.

THIS SERIES
Could change your life if it taught you how to let God
Navigate your Life!

Introduction Idea borrowed from S.E. Sangster

The 23rd Psalm

The LORD is my Shepherd;
I shall not be in want.
He makes me lie down in green pastures;
He leads me beside the still waters,
He restores my soul.
He guides me in paths of righteousness
for His name's sake.
Even though I walk through the valley of the
shadow of death, I will fear no evil,
for You are with me;
Your rod and Your staff, they comfort me.
You prepare a table before me
in the presence of my enemies.
You anoint my head with oil;
my cup runneth over.
Surely goodness and mercy will follow me
all the days of my life,
and I will dwell in the house of the LORD forever.

On A Personal Note . . .

"Lord, please keep me in Your flock and don't let me stray."

All my life, I've been a "why?" person. I drove my mother crazy with my incessant "why" questions. I was rarely satisfied with just a simple answer – I wanted details; I wanted reasoning; I wanted to know how we ended up with the answer; but most importantly – I wanted to know "why?"

Oh, to be sure, I wasn't being precocious; I just simply wanted to know "why." And so I carried that behavior right into adulthood and find myself still asking the question, "why?"

In our *Navigating Life Series*, as we dig into Psalm 23, one of the most well-known scriptures of all, the process of discovering the "why" about the author, David – King David, will be a curious adventure. I want us to bring to life the "why" behind God's choice of David the shepherd boy; the "why" along David's journey from that early, humble beginning, where at one point I have no doubt that the shepherd boy, David, wondered, "Why me, Lord?", to the ultimate, most beloved heroes of all scripture – King David. I want to discover what God saw in him – in spite of himself; why David made the choices he made; and finally, how David rested into a faith that was totally and completely dependant upon his God – the God of Israel – asking Him to be the Shepherd of his life.

And before the end of this study, we must answer the questions, "Why is this important for me and for my life today; what can I learn from him?" and "Where am I in David's journey?" You see, as we look at David's path from shepherd boy to mighty King, I believe that we will be able to pinpoint our own rights of passage along his growth chart and find that our joys, our struggles, our disappointments, our *LIFE* is truly no different than his. In fact, as we grasp the concepts of his journey, and embrace his wonderful "humanness" it will better equip us as we allow God in Christ Jesus, *THE* Shepherd, to help us navigate our lives on this earth.

Diane Parrish

A Little Historical Perspective...

Many psalms were addressed to Israel's God. Others were written about God. Psalms are commonly associated with David, King of Israel, to the point that he is usually viewed in the popular mind as the author of the complete Psalter. Although many are actually written by David, not all of them are. This genesis of this association between David and the psalms stemmed from his original position in King Saul's palace when David was one of Saul's star musicians and poet. In fact, David used his musical talents to actually sooth the horrid and alarming temper of his tormented King (Saul) when he first arrived at the palace.

Indeed there are many types of Psalms and styles – for example there are Psalms of complaint or lament, Psalms of praise and adoration, Psalms of thanksgiving, and for our study, the 23rd Psalm – Psalms of Trust.

Psalms of Trust are usually called songs of confidence and are generalized expressions of faith in God, without necessarily having a backdrop of adversity. However, it is not uncommon for them to have stemmed from a prior adverse experience.

So, before we can understand the significance of the 23rd Psalm, we must first look at the progression and journey of David's life from small shepherd boy, son of Jesse, to powerful King David, a man who left the safety of his earthly father's home, to Palace life under the watch of a mighty King. Through his journey he developed a passionate heart which yearned for nothing more than to please his Heavenly Father.

Turn to 1 Samuel and read chapter 17 and then turn to 2 Samuel, and read chapters 11 & 12.

Using those two story lines as a backdrop into our study; let's begin...

Table of Contents

Giving Up Control

Psalm 23 – Week 1 – Verse 1

The LORD is my Shepherd – I shall not want:

Lord – According to Webster's Dictionary, the word Lord means: *one having power and authority over others; a ruler by hereditary right or preeminence to whom service and obedience are due.* Although this is a Human definition of a human lord, it clearly helps to define our Heavenly God – the God of Israel of whom David writes – who has power and all authority over all and who rules by right and preeminence to whom service and obedience are truly due.

And yet, isn't it interesting that David called God his shepherd?

Shepherds have always had the most difficult job in the world. In most cultures, they have the lowest paid, least desirable job anyone could ever want. So, on a lighter note, I guess that would work for our God, because as we know for Him to shepherd His flock (you and me) it must be the most difficult thing in the universe to do! And I don't know about you, but I don't think God gets paid nearly enough for the trouble He puts up with on a daily basis (human estimation). Yet all He truly wants is simple obedience to His ways.

Let's look deeper...

Shepherds – When King David wrote, "The Lord is MY Shepherd," (emphasis, mine), he knew full well what shepherds did; who they were; and the importance of their job. After all, he had been one! He was born *INTO* that position.

Shepherds were entrusted with keeping massive groups of one of the most ignorant, least bright animals in the kingdom – Sheep. Sheep can't find food for themselves, they don't know how to find water – they don't even know if or when they need water! They can't take care of themselves; they can't fend for themselves; and yet they continue to breed flocks of ignorance!

Consider the old adage found in scripture, "lamb to the slaughter." We find it several times in our biblical texts, for example, Jeremiah 11:19 and Isaiah 53:7. In both instances, the meaning exploits the willingness of the lamb to be lead *anywhere* without argument, and without incident – almost enticing the thought, "the animal is truly ignorant of its outcome," generating the allusion of helplessness as one reads the texts.

Think about it... knowing this, David, by calling the Lord his shepherd, threw himself into the category of sheep – willing to be led, fed, helped and entrusting all outcome of his life into the hands of the shepherd.

Indeed! The ensuing relationship which develops between shepherd and flock is one of infallible trust. How did he get there and where are we in this part of the text?

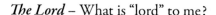

The Lord – What is "lord" to me?

What does it mean to have a "Lord?"

How does "the Lord of my life" control me? Why is it difficult to have someone else being "Lord" over our lives?

Let's look back at our Samuel texts. Clearly his brother's were jealous of him, c.f., 1 Sam 17:28ff, for there is no other reason for them to have reacted that way upon seeing David in the battle zone. Also, in the story of Bathsheba, c.f., 2 Sam 11:1ff, David took total advantage of his position, took control for SELF and abused his power to get the woman he wanted – even though she belonged to another man. And THEN, had her husband killed all for personal gain.

What sort of control issues or selfish interests did David express in the two Samuel texts? And where do I see myself in these two stories – am I capable of acting like King David?

Looking at my daily life, what sort of idyllic craziness am I subjecting myself to? Work, money, etc? How is it "lording" over me?

Is my Shepherd – Can I allow myself to have one?

The idea of God as shepherd of flocks is not unusual in the Hebrew and Testament of Jesus texts. Often Jesus referred to Himself as the Shepherd and made comments about His "sheep" no less than 45 times. The Shepherd is allegory for "caretaker" or "overseer" or even "protector." Jesus used it as hermeneutic, a means through which people would/could hear what He was saying and related it to another teaching that they understood.

What does "shepherd" mean to me?

Looking at the timeline from shepherd boy to King, when do you think David arrived at the place where he COULD call the Lord his shepherd?

Caught committing adultery and enabling an innocent man to be murdered in order to get his own way, David received his punishment. And, just as a sheep would have reacted, David did not argue with God because of the punishment (however, he did plead with God to spare the child's life). David then realized that relying on his own sinful desires and apart from God, life was not good; David, through this experience, repented of his sin and after receiving his forgiveness, allowed God to steer him back to God's flock.

As a boy, David found great joy in pleasing people and doing what they wanted in order to get attention and eventually, his own way. That served him well in the early years of young adulthood into his Kingship. But then the "want" became an insatiable abyss of need and he could no longer control his desires – they controlled him. Eventually, David learned that God truly was enough – that the things of this life were temporary – that God was eternal and that God was the ONLY thing that mattered. (c.f., II Corinthians 12:9-10)

For self reflection – here are some things to consider:

- What am I allowing to guide my steps?

- Am I fully "in" God – allowing Him to order my steps?

- Am I telling God what I want, where I want to go, and how I want to get there?

- Can I TRUST this God?

- Is my work my shepherd?

- Is my family my shepherd?

- Is the thought process, "I think I should be doing/having/spending," my shepherd?

- Is all of this creating an insatiable void?

I shall not want – What does it mean to "want," to be in need?

David had the unique advantage in life in that he was born a Shepherd boy and was thrust into the limelight (slaying Goliath), eventually becoming the King of Israel. In this era, things like this did not happen. The station in which you were born is the station in which you remained your entire life. Therefore, David knew what it meant to be "in want," and he knew what it meant to have any and everything at his fingertips.

David had to learn this lesson the hard way. What were the steps he had to endure (of his own making) in order to get to the place where he said, "I shall not want?" How about you? Where are you in this journey?

What does it mean to be satisfied – or is it a moving target?

What sort of control do "I" have over my wants, my needs, and ultimate satisfaction?

In 1988, John Armstrong wrote the song, "Pharisee." Following is the chorus:

"Now don't accuse me of heresy,
But do you think you are a Pharisee?
Does Christ have control of You,
when He does just what you tell Him to?
And do you walk by on the other side,
when a friend's in need?
Do you worry about your carpet,
while your neighbor bleeds?"

How do these words relate to you and your ability to let go of the world and cling onto God?

Therefore, if I am in control, does Christ have control of me? How do we allow God to "order our steps" and truly be the Lord of our life?

Can God be YOUR Shepherd?

Rest for the Spirit

Psalm 23 – Week 2 – Verse 2

He makes me lie down in green pastures:

IF we equate David's desire to make God his Shepherd to our own desire, and indeed IF we are to make God our Shepherd, THEN we are sheep. We are God's flock and we must do as the Shepherd says and He says for a reason.

Some things to consider about you and me: the flock. As sheep, unless we feel absolutely, completely and unquestionably safe in our surroundings, we will continue to walk until we drop over dead before we will ever allow our Shepherd to make us lie down.

Let me explain. An individual sheep is much like a baby in the womb. The baby in the womb feels secure in there because it loves the warmth, tightness, and embrace of the sides of the womb rubbing against its little body. Have you ever quickly lain down a newborn on her back only to see her "startle" as she throws her arms and legs out showing her fear? Well, so it is with sheep. Unless they feel the warmth, tightness, and sides of other sheep next to it – literally pressing up against one another – the sheep will never feel secure and never lie down and it will keep running, literally, until it either ends up dying of exhaustion from lack of water and food (it will not stop along the way to feed itself), or it runs off of a cliff or is killed by an aggressive animal.

So, in our passage, in order to be "made to lie down," I, the sheep, must feel secure – free from all fear, anxiety, and void of worry. In the Gospel of John 10:14 & 27, Jesus talks about the sheep hearing His voice and they listen and then follow. This is the ultimate trust. The sheep must *trust* the shepherd in order to feel the security that they so desperately need in order to lie down.

Now, how does that happen? How do I get to that place of "no fear?"

Can I do this on my own, or could it be that it is necessary for me to be "surrounded by other sheep in the fold" in order to feel safe and secure?

Personally, I need the structure of the "flock" in order to grow – in order to rub against me, helping me to walk the path of righteousness. You see, when I venture off on my own, outside of the confines of the flock, and into the disorderly world, it is then that I WILL, WITHOUT A DOUBT, get into trouble.

So, does God step in from time to time and cause things to happen around us in order to get our attention? Is that how He keeps us in the fold? Think that through... Or is it that by our "straying from the flock" we find ourselves in positions through which things happen, making us *want* to get back to the fold?

What about my choice? Or is it in the choice, where in God allows things to happen such that we have to lie down?

David wrote, "He makes me to lie down..." Then how does God make me do things? Better yet, WHEN can God make me do things?

And what about those green pastures?

Living sometime between 1010 and 980 B.C.E., David was born of the house of Jesse, from the tribe of Judah, in the city of Bethlehem. In other words, it was not the green-belt of produce or the rainforest! It was desert land. There was very little green, very little water, and in order to make something green, it took lots and lots of time and effort.

So, for David to use the wording, "in green pastures," that meant that he saw where God, as Shepherd, would do one of two things: 1) God would toil the earth, seed it with a seed that would produce abundant green, water the seed through the germination process and then lead David (you and me) to it, feeling in our "safe mode" and make David (you and me) lie down in the sweetness of it. That's exhausting just thinking about it. Or, 2) God would take the time to find a place and lead His flock to it so they could (all feeling in their safe zone) lie down in the sweetness of it.

Why is this so important? As the sheep grow in age, from lamb to ram or ewe, their dietary needs change as well. They need rich, green pastures in order to continue a healthy growth pattern. Ewes desperately need it for reproduction, in order to feed their own lambs (their babies). They need the nutrients from the rich, green pasture.

And so it is with the development of our faith, our Spiritual growth desperately depends on nutrition from something that only God, through Christ Jesus, can afford us (in this imagery of David) green pastures. How sad so many of us would rather eat from the dry, harsh, barren land instead of allowing the Shepherd to guide us to the land of plenty.

There can be some hindrances, for example, think about the following:
What is your definition of green pastures?

What is God's definition of "green pastures?"

How are they the same? Where are they different?

Often in the Hebrew texts (21 times) we find the imagery of "the land of Canaan – flowing with milk and honey" which conjures up pictures of richness, lushness and greenery. This image truly represents a land of plenty where no one could ever be in want.

It is this land that God promises to give to His flock – the children of Israel (the Hebrew people), and look how God lovingly and willingly wants to give it to His people. Why? Because they *need it to live* just as David (the sheep of God's flock) needed it. Just as you and I need it.

With this thought, and knowing that we don't live in the land of Canaan... What is my Canaan today?

How is God feeding me with milk and honey in the green pastures?

He leads me beside the still waters:

First, let's look at the water...

Water is essential for life. In humans about 50 to 60% of our body is comprised of water – about 1/3 of that water is what they call intercellular, meaning within the very cells of our brain, heart, vascular system, eyes, etc. In sheep, the percentage is closer to 70%. Without water neither man nor animal could survive. That is how God made us.

As a child, I remember watching the old westerns, both at the Movie Theater and on the weekly shows like *Bonanza* and *The Big Valley*. I was intrigued by the constant arguments over water. What was the big deal? There was plenty to share – so share! At least that's what my mother taught me. Of course that perspective of mine came when I was only eight years of age.

And then there were those episodes when the cowboy kept the herd from drinking from a water source because he knew that the water was not good, possibly poisoned, or could make the herd ill. I used to wonder, "How did he know the water was bad?"

So it is with our Shepherd. He not only knows that we need water to live, but where to find water. And better yet, He knows where to find water that is good for us.

Sheep, when thirsty, become restless and will literally break from the fold to find it. If sheep are not lead to the good water by the Shepherd, they will simply drink anything. Allegorically, humans will do the same thing. When not being replenished by water that fulfills the needs of the spirit, they will simply wander off in search of that which they "think" will suffice. The sad thing is, that man (sheep) can never find the good water on their own. Good water can only come from the Shepherd.

Take, for instance, the scene found in the 4th Chapter of the Gospel of John where Jesus encounters the woman from Samaria at the well. They have a conversation about water and Jesus ends up telling her the difference between "man-found water" and God-given "living water." Beginning with verse thirteen, Jesus says, "Everyone who drinks this water will be thirsty again, but whoever drinks the water I give him will never thirst. Indeed, the water I give him will become in him a spring of water welling up to eternal life."

King David eventually understood the concept of God giving living water centuries before the arrival of Christ. During his journey from having absolutely nothing to absolutely everything, David found that he could not survive without the strength of the Lord – his life's water. Indeed, upon his death bed, David's last words to his son, Solomon, were: "When the time drew near for David to die, he gave a charge to Solomon his son. 'I am about to go the way of all the earth,' he said. 'So be strong, show yourself a man, and observe what the LORD your God requires: Walk in his ways, and keep his decrees and commands, his laws and requirements, as written in the Law of Moses, so that you may prosper in all you do and wherever you go...'" (I Kings 2:1-2)

What does living water look like to you?

Why did David qualify the water as "still?"

What are the still waters?

My husband and I just returned from the lake. We have a small "run-about" boat which we purchased 25 years ago. It's amazing that it still runs with the best of them. The point is this: My least favorite times out on the lake are holiday weekends or just weekends in general. Why? Because of all the crazy people who don't know the rules of the waterways! But more importantly, on these days, I don't like being out on the boat because of all the wakes, waves and choppy water that we have to navigate through. They hurt my neck when we bounce all over the place. On those days I become tense, worried, anxious and anything but relaxed. I would much rather go at either sunset or daybreak, when the majority of the boats are put away and all that is left is the calm, quiet, hush of the stilled water.

In our daily lives, what are some ways or instances when we have to navigate "choppy waters?"

What does that look like in today's context?

Does it look like a choppy lake, or a raging ocean just before a hurricane?

What are some ways that I can access those still waters during the context of my day?

Where can I find it?

How can I make that a part of my daily journey?

Take a few moments to write down ways to enter into the still waters.

1)

2)

3)

4)

Re-Connecting to God

Psalm 23 – Week 3 – Verse 3

He restores my soul.

My Grandmother Clydie used to say, "Honey, it'll make you feel lower than a snake in a wagon-wheel-rut!" Now while this is a cute saying to describe a sad situation, the truth is, of all the highs and lows any one individual could experience, King David experienced the extremes of them all.

As a boy, he felt the hateful rejections of his older brothers (1 Samuel 17:28-30). Think about that – how many younger brothers look up to their older brothers and say to themselves, "When I grow up I want to be like him!" The truth is, there must have been some painful moments back home for David, otherwise, why would his older brother, Eliab, have reacted as he did?

Then later in life – going through the experience of the revelation of his darkest secrets; calling for and sleeping with a married woman, compounded with the follow-up action of having her husband sent to the front lines of the war simply because he found out that Bathsheba was pregnant with David's child! Feeling and acting as if he were above the law, what horrors must have filled his senses as the Prophet Nathan exposed his lies? And then, as if that weren't enough, to stand by helplessly watching as the first-born child of the woman he dearly loved dies.

Through that journey, David realized more than he wanted to. David saw himself, the ugliness of his actions and who he had become, and saw just how far removed he had taken himself from God.

- David had immense power and control as King – but God's power was greater!

- David had taken the best for himself – not for God!

- David thought himself above the law – God *IS* law.

- David concluded that God would not see that which was done in darkness – David was wrong.

- David had removed himself from God – God had not moved but was eagerly ready to receive David back to the flock.

David knew what it meant to be restored to the flock.

Centuries later, there would be another man – a man named Peter who wrote, "For you were like sheep going astray, but now you have returned to the Shepherd and Overseer of your souls." (1 Peter 2:25)

From time to time all of us find ourselves in a foreign country, even when we are right there in the confines of our own homes; our own church, or our own family. We are here, but we are not.

What were some times when you found yourself outside of the flock or in a foreign country?

How did that happen?

What did that feel like?

What made you wake up and realize that you were the one who left the flock – God didn't move?

What does a restored soul look like?

Think about this for a moment... after going to the still waters, green pastures and lying down, perhaps it is in THAT CONTEXT wherein our souls are finally restored?

What are your thoughts on this?

You see David realized that unless he totally trusted in God, allowed himself to be lead to the green pastures by God so he could completely relax, and then was willing to listen fully to that which God wanted to do with his life, his spirit could not be restored to God.

And so in that moment David's spirit received his salvation – the salvation of a lost soul. It is true, throughout his whole life, David was a man after God's own heart, but it wasn't until this moment wherein David realized that he had not been willing to go "all in." And isn't that then the purpose of this Psalm, the description of a saved soul's understanding, that David wanted future generations to embrace?

Through our salvation, our spirit is restored to God. And then in the text that follows, David reveals to the hearer and singer of the Psalm the reason why our souls are not restored for our sake alone – rather for God's sake.

He guides me in paths of righteousness for His name's sake.

I love the positioning of this sentence in David's Psalm. He could have placed it anywhere and we (the readers) would not have thought anything about it.

Several years ago while serving on a Clergy team for a Walk to Emmaus weekend, in his talk, one of the Spiritual Directors made the statement, "ruts are nothing more than coffins with both ends knocked out." I kind of liked that statement. And it fits here. Just how many times do we as Christians decide to change our own paths? We vow at the New Year to change a habit, and/or we declare to God that we promise that, "...we will never do that again!"

You see, we, like sheep, prefer patterns and will remain in them until we are "made" to do something differently by their Shepherd. It has something to do with trust – self trust. When sheep venture away from the flock, and find an area they like, they choose to stay there and WILL stay there literally until they die. Why? Because they trust and feel safe in the new area and want to remain there, and they do.

Patterns, habits, ruts are nothing more than coffins with both ends knocked out. God knows this. David learned this. David had taken the reins of his own life and decided that he knew what was better for himself than God. Like a wandering sheep, David had left the flock and ventured into his own, self-made area. There he remained for quite a while, making many poor choices, and closing his spirit to God, all the while sinking lower and lower until he came to the emotional/spiritual place in which he finally allowed himself to listen to his Shepherd and place his complete trust in Him once again.

Take a few moments and think of some of your personal habits, patterns and/or ruts that you know you are following.

How are these keeping you from a "complete" trusting relationship with God?

What steps do you think you need to take in order to incline your spirit towards God to hear His voice and lead you?

Paths of righteousness:

Did anyone pick up on the subtlety of David's words here? Did you notice that David wrote, "Paths OF righteousness" and not "Paths TO righteousness?" Most folks twist this in their minds – I know I did for years until one day it hit me over the head! Pure righteousness – as a human I will never achieve while here on earth. So, while on earth, I can not become pure righteous – only Jesus Christ was pure righteousness.

You see, even though I will not *ever become* purely righteous, it is something that I strive for, that I yearn for with the help of my Savior Jesus Christ working in/on me daily. But on my own, I can not achieve pure righteousness. John Wesley called that Sanctifying Grace – where the grace of God, in Jesus Christ, works IN US daily, rooting out our sinfulness through paths of righteousness. I can not do this on my own!

What David writes here is that it is all about the journey from point "A" to point "whatever." It is the journey, our journey *on the paths of righteousness*, willing to be led by the Shepherd, wherein we find God's plans and fulfillment of life.

Indeed, if left on their own, sheep are lousy at managing themselves. They need to be managed, skillfully managed on safe paths, healthy paths, on *righteous paths*. David knew this as a former shepherd. He knew what it took to manage a flock of sheep, a job that knew no rest. A shepherd has to have a predetermined, safe and healthy plan implemented at all times in order to move the sheep from one place to another. There can be nothing random about shepherding sheep.

Did I mention before that sheep are considered to be one of the least smart animals? And did I mention that in this Psalm, David allowed himself to become the sheep in order to have God as his Shepherd? Just a reminder.

Yes, and so in the sheep mode – you and I need someone to manage our daily existence *on the paths of* righteousness. We need:

- Someone with a master plan.
- Someone who has the best intentions for our lives.
- Someone who has studied the terrain and knows where to take us to find the green pastures and the best pools of water for drinking.
- Someone who knows when we need rest.
- Someone who has looked out into eternity, sees where we are heading and does everything to get us back on path with Him so we don't fall off of the cliff.

And that Shepherd will lead us in good paths, in righteous paths to ensure our safe arrival at the destination place in the master plan – Eternal life with God.

Righteousness, not perfection, is listed over 300 times in our Biblical Cannon. So it must be important to God. If you look at some of the righteous men in the Bible you see those who desperately seek God's heart – and yet – in spite of their attempts, fall short and mess up from time to time. True, they are striving for perfection, but ask yourself this: Are they striving for perfection to "impress or to please God" by doing so on their own? Or, are they truly allowing God to "lead them in paths of righteousness?"

God's thoughts on His paths of righteousness are different from my self-imposed paths. Following are some of the tributes to God's paths of righteousness found in Paul's letter to the churches in Galatia.

― ・ ― ・ ―

"22 But the fruit of the Spirit is love, joy, peace, patience, kindness, goodness, faithfulness, 23 gentleness and self-control. Against such things there is no law. 24 Those who belong to Christ Jesus have crucified the sinful nature with its passions and desires." (Galatians 5:22-23)

"2 Carry each other's burdens, and in this way you will fulfill the law of Christ." 3 If anyone thinks he is something when he is nothing, he deceives himself. 4 Each one should test his own actions. Then he can take pride in himself, without comparing himself to somebody else, 5 for each one should carry his own load. 6 Anyone who receives instruction in the word must share all good things with his instructor. 7 Do not be deceived: God cannot be mocked. A man reaps what he sows. 8 The one who sows to please his sinful nature, from that nature will reap destruction; the one who sows to please the Spirit, from the Spirit will reap eternal life. 9 Let us not become weary in doing good, for at the proper time we will reap a harvest if we do not give up. 10 Therefore, as we have opportunity, let us do good to all people, especially to those who belong to the family of believers. (Galatians 6:2-10)

Take a few moments to write down your thoughts on what "paths of righteousness" look like. In other words, how can you implement Paul's words into your own life on a daily basis?

What do they include?

What do they try to navigate away from?

For His Name's sake

To me, this is one of the most difficult sections of the 23rd Psalm. Never in all my years in the Life of the Church, have I ever heard a sermon on these four words, "for His Name's sake." You see, all my life, I thought I was to be lead in paths of righteousness in order for me to get to heaven. But NO! That is not what David wrote. David wrote that I am led down paths of righteousness not for "my sake" RATHER for "God's sake."

How is that different? Well, if I am led for my sake, then it becomes all about me. However, if I am lead for God's Name's sake, then it is all about Him. And while one could argue that these two processes ultimately lead to the same outcome, the bottom line is that IF I am one of God's sheep, then I have His brand; I have His label. Therefore, I MUST represent Him in all situations, at all times, and at all cost.

Think about this with me: IF we are to be called the People of God, God's sheep, then we must be led down paths of righteousness to do honor to God – our salvation, while primary for eternity, becomes secondary while living on earth. Our salvation becomes a by-product of God's purpose for us while here, thus the wording, "for His Name's sake."

Several times over my years of teaching and preaching God's word, people have heard me say, that my salvation is not for me alone – my salvation is for all the people I come into contact with for GOD'S SAKE. If my salvation is simply for me, then how would anyone else ever hear about the "path" to righteousness, the "path" to salvation UNLESS someone took the time to tell you or me about it?

David knew that people saw his fall from Grace, and it was vitally important to David that people see his RESTORATION back into the fold of God's flock. To David, people needed to see that God, THE Shepherd, will never, ever leave His flock alone – that they are safe in the protection of the Shepherd. After all, they carry God's own Name. To God, He needed David to guide others through his Psalms and through his leadership, but most importantly, to God, He needed David to be a living example so that

OTHERS could come to know David's Shepherd – the God of Israel.
Take a few moments to write down and discuss the "why" of your salvation not only for yourself, rather for all those around you and who come into contact with you.

Peaceful Confidence

Psalm 23 – Week 4 – Verse 4

Even though I walk through the valley of the shadow of death;

I remember a family vacation that my husband and I took with our two children. The kids were in their early teens, my husband was getting ready to go to work for another company, I was on a leave of absence from the local Church to develop a ministry, and we had a little extra time off. So we rented an RV, loaded up the kids and set out for a three-week vacation exploring the Wild West. Oh, the memories we made!

One particular memory was the day my daughter and I signed up with a ranch to move some longhorn steer (cattle) from one side of the ranch to the other. Having grown up riding horses, we were excited about this all-day event and knew we would have fun.

Well, I wouldn't exactly jump to "fun!" It was probably one of the most difficult things we had ever done on horseback. I might want to argue with the source that places sheep at the bottom of the brain department and place longhorn cows there! The point is – we had to watch each one of them. The steers on the outer edge of the herd would just run off and we had to chase them down and get them back to the herd.

The reason I bring this story to your attention is for this reason. While on our adventure with the cows, my daughter and I experienced perfect weather, and pretty much close to perfect terrain. We did not have any cliffs to worry about. We didn't have to "bed the steer down" for the night. Nor did we have to journey with the cattle from one season to another over a long period of time enduring scorching heat and freezing cold. And so, if we are the sheep on this journey, we MUST acknowledge that even while on the path with the Shepherd, in the safety of His keeping, there will be times where, in addition to the good, we will experience the hazards as well; the difficulties of it, the dangers of wolves coming to steel us away, and the scariness of the unknown.

Up to this point in the Psalm, David has only described the roles of the sheep and the Shepherd. He has established who we are and who our Shepherd is. We get that we are to follow His lead, listen to His voice, and keep close to the fold. But until now, David has not addressed the why or where we are on the journey.

And so it is here, in verse four wherein David begins to acknowledge the thoughts, emotions and realizations of the sheep in the context of their journey. We are able to see just how far they have come in their TRUST of the Shepherd as they follow Him in paths of righteousness.

Even though I walk through the valley of the shadow of death… For a sheep, the shadow of death is like looking up from grazing in the green pasture and seeing a wolf staring it right in the eyes. That's "the shadow of death!"

Looking back at our two Samuel texts, where was David's valley of the shadow of death? Where was he staring the wolf right in the eye?

And how about you? Think back over your life where the wolf was staring you right in the eye. What did that look like?

We can not do it on our own.
We can not find our own paths.
We can not save ourselves from the wolf.

We MUST trust the Shepherd to lead us as we listen to His voice.

I will fear no evil, for You are with me;

After establishing the "scary" part, David quickly resolves the matter by acknowledging the role of the Shepherd in the context, thus alleviating the "fear" part. Upon seeing the wolf, the instinct of the sheep is to "bleep" out a distress call. Upon hearing the bleep, the Shepherd immediately comes to the rescue, therefore, "I will fear no evil."

For example in the 14th Chapter of Matthew, beginning with verse 25, we see where Jesus comes to the rescue of Peter while He is leading them along paths of righteousness as their Shepherd:

---

25 During the fourth watch of the night Jesus went out to them, walking on the lake. 26 When the disciples saw Him walking on the lake, they were terrified. "It's a ghost," they said, and cried out in fear. 27 But Jesus immediately said to them: "Take courage! It is I. Don't be afraid." 28 "Lord, if it's you," Peter replied, "tell me to come to you on the water." 29 "Come," He said. Then Peter got down out of the boat, walked on the water and came toward Jesus. 30 But when he saw the wind, he was afraid and, beginning to sink, cried out, **"Lord, save me!"** 31 **Immediately** Jesus reached out His hand and caught him. "You of little faith," He said, "why did you doubt?"

In verse 30 we see where Peter, having followed the Shepherd out onto the water, *stops* trusting the Shepherd, decides to take matters into his own hands and therefore begins to sink.

When did Peter "bleep" out the distress call?

When did the Shepherd come to the rescue? How long did it take the Shepherd to come to the rescue?

Take note here: Jesus, having already established the fact that He is the Shepherd of His flock (10th Chapter of John's Gospel), chastises Peter for not trusting. This is so fundamental to the Disciples' understanding of what it means to trust the Shepherd, to trust the voice of God, and not listen to the challenges of this world.

Jesus had already determined that Peter would be the "rock on which He would build the Church of God" (Matthew 16:18). So Christ deemed it was necessary to challenge Peter on his faith to ensure that Peter understood that the reason he started to sink was because he had doubted his own faith and the ability of the Shepherd to lead him. And then later, knowing that Peter would stray from his faith and ultimately get restored, Jesus says, "But I have prayed for you, Simon, that your faith may not fail. And when you have turned back, strengthen your brothers." (Luke 22:32)

Peter wasn't the first one to be challenged with this faith. Think about these two men: Noah and Abraham. When was the last time you built a major arc in the middle of the desert with no modern equipment? And when was the last time God asked you to take your beloved son to the mountain and sacrifice him?

In his second letter to his disciple, Timothy, as encouragement, the Apostle Paul wrote, "For God did not give us a spirit of timidity, but a spirit of power, of love and of self-discipline." (II Timothy 1:7) God does not want a spirit of timidity, rather a bold spirit in stark contrast to anything the world throws our way.

God did not want David to have a spirit of timidity – God needed a restored David to be strong of faith and to lead Israel.

Jesus did not want Peter to have a spirit of timidity – Jesus needed a restored Peter to become the rock on which God's church would grow.

Paul did not want young Timothy to have a spirit of timidity – Even though Timothy was young in years, Paul needed him to be secure in his faith as he lead the people to Christ in that region.

In today's context what is fear? What are ways we exercise fear in our daily life?

HOW do we get to the point where we are strong in our faith and secure in the keeping of our Shepherd that no matter what we face, we will not fear any evil?

Your rod and Your staff, they comfort me;

All of us in God's flock are on different journeys. Some of us have pondered what it must be like to journey outside of the flock and have great fear of that unknown. Therefore, we stay fast within the safety net of the flock with our friends and family standing near. Others of us have challenged the confines of the flock finding it necessary to journey off on our own and into foreign territory only to lose our way and everything we held dear, before allowing the Shepherd to woo us back to the herd.

Having been saved by the outstretched hand of the Shepherd, David realized just how far he had strayed and wanted to ensure that his sons and future Israeli generations did not follow the path he had travelled. Because of his life choices, David found that the comfort inside the safety net of the herd was ever so much sweeter than any self-fulfilled desire of his flesh.

What are some of the ways you find comfort in your Savior?

God Celebrating His Child

Psalm 23 – Week 5 – Verse 5

You prepare a table before me

It is difficult to think about herds of sheep without thinking about terrain. Clearly in the geographical area in which David lived, he endured mountainous landscapes as well as valleys and everything in between.

For David to use the wording, *prepare a table before me*, brings to light two schools of thoughts in my mind. Could it be that he used a double entendre'?

The first thought of the table preparation is simply that, preparing a table for me. That God would take the time to prepare a table filled with abundant food - for me. Shouldn't it be the other way around? Shouldn't I be the one preparing a table of food for my Shepherd? Not according to

David. You see, keeping it in context, to prepare a table of food in that era was a huge task. One simply did not run to the grocery store, grab a cart, fill it up with many pre-made entrée's, head back to the house, and cook. NO! Food took long, tedious hours of planning, preparation, mixing, and putting together that which was planned. And the host always anguished over the outcome – would it be acceptable? Will it turn out right? Is the harvest ripe for the produce I need? To get a glance of the anxiety level, all one has to do is read Luke's account of when Jesus and His Disciples came to visit the house of Martha and Mary in Chapter 10, verses 38 and following.

This type of table preparation was an all day event – to break the fast, the cook started the preparation time around 3:00 in the morning (about three hours before sunrise). For the mid-day meal, the preparation began while the breakfast meal was being served! And the last meal of the day took sometimes six hours to prepare! And to think that the God of Israel, *his* SHEPHERD would do that for him, was overwhelming to David. Yet he knew that God would do that for him.

What about you? Do you think God would do that for you?

Think back over your journey so far, where were times when you know God did something for you? What did that look like? How did that make you feel?

The second thought regarding table preparation takes on another course altogether. The etymology of the word table stems from the Latin word Mensa, from which the Spanish word, mesa comes. A table or mesa in geographical terms simply means an upper layer or plateau within a mountainous region. It could mean large spans of flat or gently sloping terrain – much desired when herding weary sheep.

If the Shepherd wants to make the sheep lie down in green pastures in order to give them rest he must first find a mesa or plateau.

When He finds what He is looking for, He will prepare the ground for the sheep through many tasks. For example, he will ensure that there is plenty of water, he will rid the land of anything which could harm the sheep (fill in holes, rid the land of poisonous plants, aggressive animals) and He will determine the strength of the land, (where the grass is weakest, and where it is more abundant). In other words – the Shepherd makes sure that the land will support the life of the herd before He ever decides to take them there.

When our daughter was less than two years of age, she drove us nuts. Absolutely EVERYTHING that she touched, pressed up against, picked up – if it could fit into her hand – it went into her mouth! If we sat her in her high chair – she would bend over and try to smell the tray! If she was curious about ANYTHING – she either tasted it or smelled it. What a wonderfully, inquisitive child! How she lived beyond those first 24 months of age was truly a gift from God!

The point is this – her daddy and I had to prepare every single room, seat, and play area that we would place her in because if we didn't she could seriously hurt herself. We as Christians are like that, too. We will try anything, we will taste everything, and we will even venture into unsafe lands out of either ignorance or defiance (depending on where we are on our journey)! God knows His sheep, and it is for that very reason that God goes before us and prepares for our arrival. David knew this and wrote about it. And before Jesus departed from this earth, He told His Disciples that He would go to prepare a place for them in heaven, (c.f. John 14:2-3).

So with this second thought in mind – what are some ways that you can now see where God had actually gone before you to prepare the way for you? (c.f., Deuteronomy 1:30)

Could it have been with work?

Could it have been a relationship?

What are some ways?

...in the presence of my enemies,

Where I grew up in mid-state Florida, there were no other girls in my neighborhood. How that happened, I have no idea. So, if I wanted to play outside with anyone, I had to play with boys! I had to run like them, kick like them, and play sports like them and obviously, I prayed everyday for God to send girls! Anyway, my two best friends were David and Stevie. Man, the three of us could get into more trouble than any kids around.

I remember this one Friday afternoon. My father had just come home from work which meant my sister and I had to be inside. I don't know why – we just had to. On this particular day, dad had come home with a headache and was lying down. Stevie and David wanted me to come out and play in the neighborhood. They needed me to round out a kick-ball team. Since I couldn't go, they decided to pull a prank. They ran up to the front door, rang the doorbell two times and then ran like rabbits to the woods next door. Well, after they did this a couple of times, needless to say, Dad was not too happy. So, he waited for the next time and then just before they reached up to ring the doorbell, dad quickly opened the door and said, "May I help you?"

The boys took off running, scared to death of the wrath of Bob! Dad yelled after them to come back. David just kept running. But Stevie heard the tone in dad's voice and determined that the better part of "personal salvation" would be to come back to our house. Watching Stevie through the front picture window, I thought to myself, "Gee, Stevie, you should have kept running!" And our friend David was yelling back to Stevie calling him a traitor friend.

Then my dad did the most amazing thing. He said, "Stevie because you came back when I called you, would you like a bowl of ice cream?" Shocked beyond belief, he eked out a, "Yes, sir." So my dad made him a humongous bowl of ice cream, placed a stool smack dab in the middle of the picture window at the front of our house, set Stevie up on it, and gave him the ice cream. Stevie was on display for the world to see.

Just then, peering out from the woods, my friend David saw that dad had given Stevie ice cream and thinking that looked pretty good, he came back to the house and inquired of my dad if he, too, could have some. Dad said, "Well David, you know Stevie came back when I called him. And because of that, I gave him ice cream as his reward. But sadly you ran away instead and ignored my call, therefore, you can not have any. Perhaps next time you will think this through..."

The point? My dad prepared a bowl of ice cream for Stevie in the presence of his angry buddy. Even though Stevie, too, had done wrong, by his returning, my dad restored him to good wishes and good standing in our household in the presence of those who chose not to.

Looking back over this story – where are you in it? Are you Diane, saying, "gee, you should have kept running;" Stevie, returning to the scene of that which he did wrong; or are you David, still running?

Surely in your journey you have encountered similar situations – what did they look like? Who got restored? How did they feel about being restored?

You anoint my head with oil;

In the Hebrew faith, oil is used for two main purposes – to consecrate those going into ministry or for some mission and as a healing balm for anything from war injuries to birth pains and anything else which caused physical pain.

I believe that David intended for both purposes to be considered. That is to say, by using the *anointing with oil* motif, David states that God will consecrate us for His purposes (remember: for His Name's sake), and then will keep us healthy.

What does that mean to us, God's sheep? Well, have you ever had an itch in the middle of your back and there was no one there to scratch it for you? Me? I grab whatever I can get my hands on and keep pushing it up and down my back until the itch goes away. Now, as a human, I kind of know when to stop – if it hurts I will stop. Sheep won't. They don't know to. They will keep working something until it gets bruised, cut, or rubbed raw.

One of the most disturbing things to sheep are insects, flies, gnats – you name them – they irritate sheep to craziness. In the heat of the summer, flies will attack the eyes, the nose and the edges of the mouths in order to get water from the animal. And if there is an open wound? Pay dirt! But these open wounds quickly turn to a disease called scab and it spreads from sheep to sheep – many of whom succumb to it.

The insects annoy the sheep so much that often they stop eating, they become anxious and lose trust in their surroundings causing them to wander off. The only recourse the sheep has is to rub its head against something, or against another sheep's head, until the flies are all smashed. But this is only temporary because there's another round of flies just around the ear from the face, ready to pounce once again. Sheep will literally go to battle with another sheep while in the confines of the herd if it means they get temporary relief from their misery. Shepherds know this. So, in order to keep the insects at bay and away, the Shepherd anoints the sheep's head with oil. The perfumes in the oil will drive the flies and insects away giving much needed relief to the sheep.

Guess how many times the Shepherd needs to do this? Once only? NO! Because daily attention is given to His sheep the Shepherd will do this as often as is needed. There is no such thing as "once anointed, always anointed." What I mean by that is this – one application of oil will not withstand the elements of weather day in and day out. To be sure, the storms of life and rubbing heads with other sheep will reduce the oil's sustainability and effectiveness. The Shepherd must reapply often.

So it is with us. When something isn't going our way, when things are irritating us, bothering us, destroying the very moments of our lives, do we have the presence of mind to turn to the Shepherd for help or do we try to "work it" on our own? (Remember the ruts?)

What does that look like to you?

When have you tried to solve it all by yourself without the healing oil from the Shepherd?

And before the question comes out from your mouth – I am not talking about salvation here. Just like the sheep are always a part of the Shepherd's flock, so are we a part of the Shepherd's flock. What I'm talking about here is the reapplying, the maintenance, the replenishing of the oil that is readily available for those – if we will only ask, seek and then receive.

What are some times when you needed refilling?

...my cup overflows.

Keep in mind that the journey for the Shepherd and the sheep not only navigate through a changing terrain, but it endures drastic changes in weather as well. Within a years' time, they will travel through temperatures ranging from 100 degrees Fahrenheit to 10 degrees Fahrenheit. Because of this swing in temperature, the sheep's coat will grow until it can sustain the sheep in the freezing winters. However, because of the weight and thickness of the coat, the sheep have trouble walking so the Shepherd must cut it off. In other words, it must be pruned. The sheep's wool is used to help with many human needs as well. It is used to weave clothing and blankets. It is also used as a sort of stuffing for pillows or bedding.

What about the cup? Well the image of overflowing conjures up thoughts of plenty, abundance, more than one could ever use all up.

On the journey, water and wine are staples for the Shepherd. It is not unusual for the Shepherd to share His wine with a sick or freezing lamb. The wine brings warmth to the body of the lamb, and his life is restored. As scarce as these elements are, the Shepherd will not hesitate to give them to His flock if they are in need.

Again, we see ourselves in this imagery of the Shepherd giving us drink in abundance, overflowing the very rim of our cup, spilling onto the table or ground. And it is in this very overflowing wherein we realize that there is more than enough for us and more than enough for anyone who would be in want of the cup of the Shepherd.

——————————— • • ———————————

> "15 And He said to them, "I have eagerly desired to eat this Passover with you before I suffer. 16 For I tell you, I will not eat it again until it finds fulfillment in the kingdom of God." 17 After taking the cup, He gave thanks and said, "Take this and divide it among you. 18 For I tell you I will not drink again of the fruit of the vine until the kingdom of God comes." 19 And He took bread, gave thanks and broke it, and gave it to them, saying, "This is my body given for you; do this in remembrance of me." 20 In the same way, after the supper He took the cup, saying, "This cup is the new covenant in my blood, which is poured out for you." (Luke 22:15-20)

When have you experienced the abundance of the cup of life that Jesus offers you?

How has that manifested itself in your daily life?

Blessed Eternal Assurance

Psalm 23 – Week 6 – Verse 6

Surely goodness and mercy will follow me all the days of my life, and I will dwell in the house of the Lord, forever.

Just as the Shepherd left the 99 sheep to find the one lost one (Luke 15:1-7); just as the lost coin was found by the woman (Luke 15:8-10); just as the prodigal son returned to the jubilant, outstretched arms of his father (Luke 15:11-32); so we too must feel the redemptive love God has for us as we ponder the words that God spoke to us through the prophet Isaiah:

> ""Remember not the events of the past, the things of long ago consider not; See, I am doing something new! Now it springs forth, do you not perceive it?" (Isaiah 43:18-19)

"It is I, I, who wipe out, for my own sake, your offenses; your sins I remember no more." (Isaiah 43:25)

"I have brushed away your offenses like a cloud, your sins like a mist; return to me, for I have redeemed you." (Isaiah 44:22)

"Return to me and be safe, all you ends of the earth, for I am God; there is no other!" (Isaiah 45:22)

We have been redeemed through the grace and mercy of a Sovereign Shepherd. A Shepherd who watches our every move, hears our every thought, and feels our every breath. Our redemption has nothing to do with anything that we do; rather it has everything to do with what God says about us – what God wants FOR US.

You see, when we walk in the paths laid out for us by the Shepherd, we walk in paths of righteousness. And then by so doing, the grace and mercy of our God will surround us; it will go before us and clean up after us.

In his letter to the churches in Ephesus, Paul writes, "For it is by grace you have been saved, through faith--and this not from yourselves, it is the gift of God – not by works, so that no one can boast," (Ephesians 2:8-9). Nothing we can do will ever earn our salvation. Nothing we can do will ever earn our way into heaven. It is totally and absolutely only through the grace and mercy offered to us by God through Christ that we get to spend eternity with our Savior.

What are some of the ways that you see where people are trying to work their way into heaven?

Why aren't works good enough? Where do we fall short?

Think about this for a moment – now that we have come to the end of our Psalm – what do you think about the following statement?

— • • —

"According to me, I know that I don't deserve to
be in heaven with God, but for some reason God
seems to think so."
(Isaiah 49:1-5 & 8-10 & 15-16; Exodus 13:9 & 16;
and Deuteronomy 6:4-9)

Take a few moments to ponder that statement.

How do you think David would respond to that statement?

Do you think he felt as if he deserved to be restored?

I do and here's why. In spite of us, while we were yet sinners, God chose to love us back to the flock. When we strayed, when we did the very things that we were ordered not to do, to the point where God Himself could not even look at us – He redeemed us. When the indescribable had to be done,

God did not send an angel, He did not send a prophet – God sent His son to redeem a fallen world; that whosoever would believe in Him would not perish, but would indeed have eternal life – redeemed ONLY by His blood. Therefore, God decided that we deserved to be redeemed, not of our own doing, rather of His doing.

David knew this. David knew this long before Jesus ever came to this earth. He knew that his Shepherd, the Almighty God of Israel had nothing better to do one day than to reach down into this miry, muck of a sinful world and grab David up by the lapel and say, "David, boy, YOU ARE MINE for all eternity!" David didn't need to know how God was going to do that. He didn't need to know if God would come through with His promise.

No, David didn't need any of those things. David had taken the journey from having nothing to having everything and at the end of the day, the ONLY THING that mattered to him was that his Shepherd cared for him. In each of the following, where are you in your understanding of David's realizations?

The Lord is my shepherd – David, yielding his own stature in life to God, acknowledged this to the entire Hebrew nation.

I shall not want – showing that stuff in life didn't matter nearly as much as God's love and direction. It was all David could ever need.

He makes me lie down in green pastures – putting his whole trust in God as his Shepherd, David knew how to let God make him rest, and he shared it with others.

He leads me beside the still waters – showing that only God can calm the storms of life.

He restores my soul – David experienced first hand that only God can restore the brokenness of the human spirit.

He guides me in paths of righteousness – David learned that his paths lead to disaster, and that the paths of God are always pure and Holy; I will follow His paths.

For His Name's sake – that I belong to God, I am His and He is mine – all that I am is for the Glory of God.

Even though I walk through the valley of the shadow of death – On this earth we will encounter trouble, evil and sadness. David acknowledged this and trusted God to lead him through.

I will fear no evil for you are with me – How can I be afraid of anything when the God of the universe is my Shepherd, ordering my daily steps?

Your rod and Your staff, they comfort me – In the middle of raging storms, you will come and comfort me. David learned that he will never be alone.

You prepare a table before me in the presence of my enemies – David learned that God will restore His flock and in the presence of all those who hated him, God will flaunt His flock.

You anoint my head with oil – The healing balm of God far outweighs anything of this world. God will protect His flock from evil at all cost – even at the expense of His own Son's life.

My cup runneth over – David experienced the unending, unwavering love of his Shepherd – it was abundant and everlasting.

Surely goodness and mercy will follow me all the days of my life – it wasn't always that way with David – but he knew that from this day forward, that God would cover him with goodness and mercy and restore David to right relationship with God.

And I will dwell in the house of the Lord, forever – David knew that life on earth is temporary – but that the House of the Lord is for all eternity. David ended his life in total peace knowing that he would indeed live in the House of the Lord for all eternity – he had this assurance.

How about you? Have you come to the place in your life where you have placed your total and complete trust in the Shepherd allowing Him to order your steps in paths of righteousness for His sake?

If you are still unsure, how I pray you will take the time to talk to God asking Him to help you in your understanding. And how I pray that you will ask Him into your heart, to order your steps, and to become the Lord (Shepherd) of your life so that you can live in the House of the Lord forever!

It's never too late, you know!

About the Author...

With a fervent love for her Savior, Jesus Christ – Diane embraces life and all the challenges therein with joy and great anticipation.

After graduating from the University of Florida with Honors in Music Theory and Composition, Diane took a prodigal run to Hollywood. There, totally away from the Church, she wanted desperately to become a "somebody." And she did. She became a well known musical arranger, lead background singer for Tony Orlando and worked with named stars like Barry Manilow, Melissa Manchester, Danny Thomas on his "St. Jude Telethons," and John Davidson... Until the morning God made her HIS somebody and whispered, "Diane, come home."

...so she did. There she met and married the human love of her life – Raymond Parrish. After thirty years of marriage, two kids, three dogs, three cats, 24 puppies, hamsters and sea monkeys in a jar on her windowsill in the kitchen – ask her and she'll tell you, "Life doesn't get much better than this!"

An Elder with the United Methodist Church, Diane is a well-known author, speaker and retreat leader in the Southeastern Jurisdiction. Her gifts for humor, as well as the depth of her faith and biblical knowledge, serve well to encourage people along their faith journey and introduction to Christ.

Diane founded kidz2leaders, Inc.® a 501(c)(3) corporation with special ministries including Camp Hope® – camps for the 4th, 5th and 6th grade children of incarcerated parents, the Leadership Training Academy – the second tier of Camp Hope® for middle-school ages, hope4christmas® our annual Christmas event, and interns4tomorrow®, preparing our teenage campers for their future in Corporate America, breaking the dependency factor.

As you journey through this bible study, enjoy the passion of a woman saved by grace and set apart by God for...well, she's not sure yet, but the expedition is thrilling!